ANIMALS AT A GLANCE
WILD ANIMALS

For a free color catalog describing Gareth Stevens' list of high-quality books, call 1-800-542-2595 (USA) or 1-800-461-9120 (Canada). Gareth Stevens' Fax: (414) 225-0377.

The editor would like to thank Elizabeth S. Frank, Curator of Large Mammals at the Milwaukee County Zoo, Milwaukee, Wisconsin, for her kind and professional assistance regarding the accuracy of information in this book.

Library of Congress Cataloging-in-Publication Data

Baierlacher, Monika.
  [Aus aller Welt. English]
  Wild animals / by Monika Baierlacher ; illustrated by Christoph Scholl.
    p. cm. -- (Animals at a glance)
  Includes index.
  ISBN 0-8368-1355-3
  1. Animals--Juvenile literature. [1. Animals.] I. Scholl,
Christoph, ill. II. Title. III. Series: Lerne Tiere kennen.
English.
QL49.B12713 1995
591--dc20   95-13964

This edition first published in 1996 by
Gareth Stevens Publishing
1555 North RiverCenter Drive, Suite 201
Milwaukee, Wisconsin 53212, USA

This edition © 1996 by Gareth Stevens, Inc. Original edition published in 1996 by Mangold Verlag, LDV Datenverabeitung Gesellschaft m. b. H, A-8042 Graz, St-Peter-Hauptstrasse 28, Austria, under the title **Lerne Tiere Kennen-Aus Aller Welt.** Text © 1996 by Monika Baierlacher. Illustrations © 1996 by Christoph Scholl. Additional end matter © 1996 by Gareth Stevens, Inc.

Series editor: Barbara J. Behm
Editorial assistants: Diana L. Kahn, Diane Laska
Logo design: Helene Feider

Printed in Mexico

1 2 3 4 5 6 7 8 9 99 98 97 96

ANIMALS AT A GLANCE
WILD ANIMALS

by MONIKA BAIERLACHER
Illustrated by CHRISTOPH SCHOLL

The **Koala** is a marsupial. When marsupials are born, they are tiny and underdeveloped. They finish growing in a pouch on their mother's belly.

Height: 24-33 inches
(61-84 centimeters)
Weight: 9-29 pounds
(4-13 kilograms)
Diet: Eucalyptus leaves
Location: Australia
Lifespan: 13 years

Newborn grows for six months in mother's pouch

Good sense of smell

Fluffy coat

Second and third back toes are grown together

Sharp, hook-shaped claws for climbing

Thumb for grasping

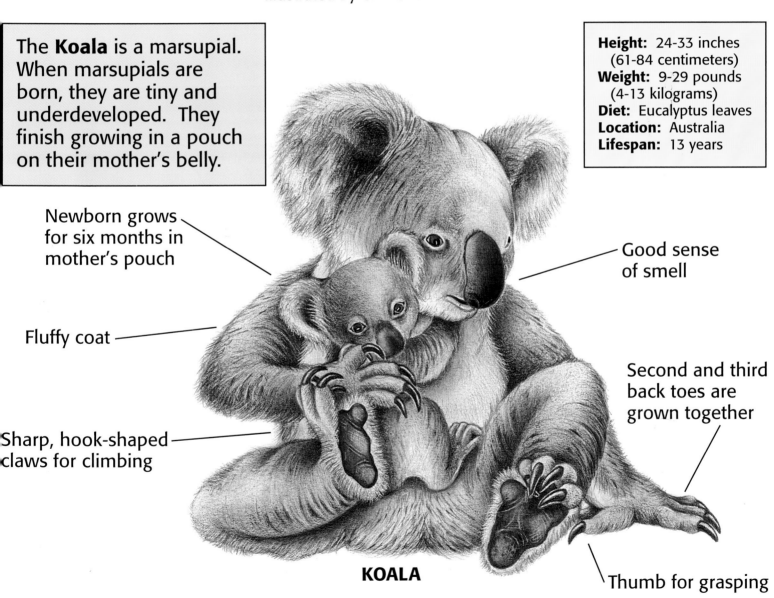

KOALA

Gareth Stevens Publishing
MILWAUKEE

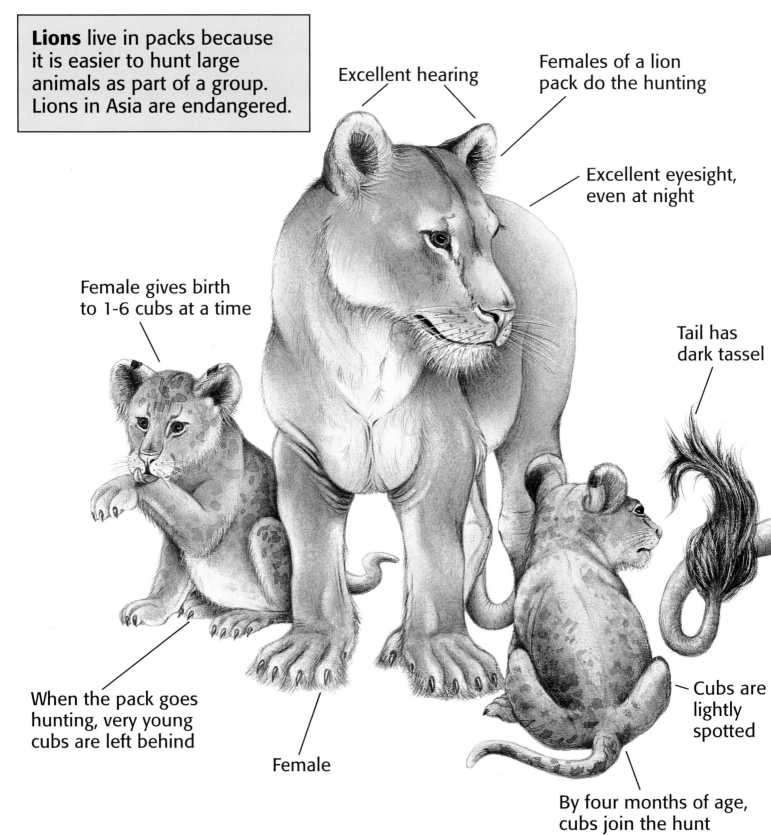

Lions live in packs because it is easier to hunt large animals as part of a group. Lions in Asia are endangered.

Excellent hearing

Females of a lion pack do the hunting

Excellent eyesight, even at night

Tail has dark tassel

Female gives birth to 1-6 cubs at a time

When the pack goes hunting, very young cubs are left behind

Female

Cubs are lightly spotted

By four months of age, cubs join the hunt

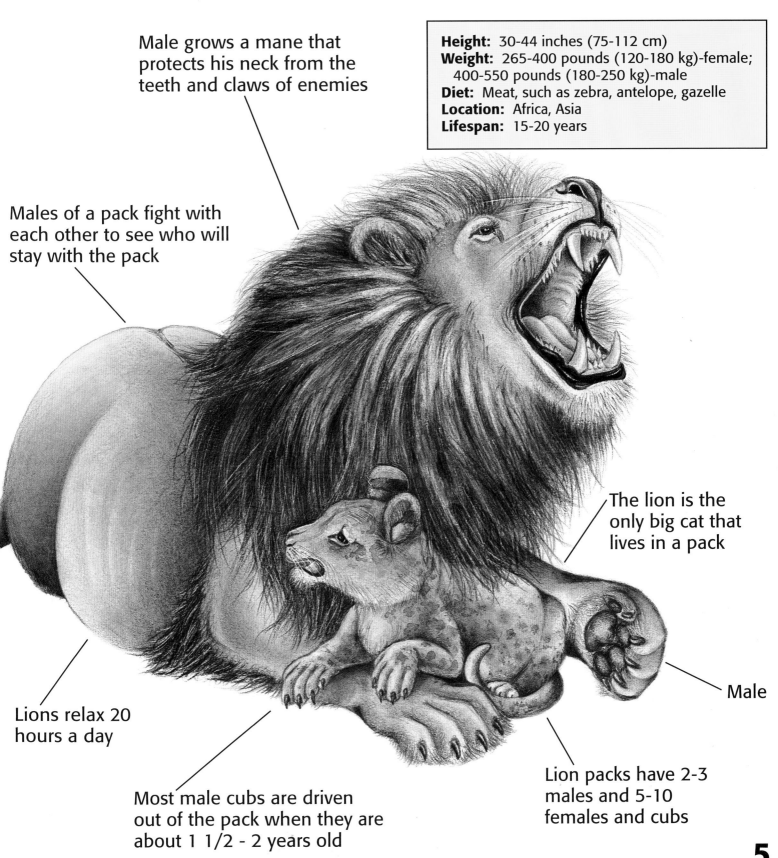

Male grows a mane that protects his neck from the teeth and claws of enemies

Males of a pack fight with each other to see who will stay with the pack

Lions relax 20 hours a day

Most male cubs are driven out of the pack when they are about 1 1/2 - 2 years old

Height: 30-44 inches (75-112 cm)
Weight: 265-400 pounds (120-180 kg)-female;
400-550 pounds (180-250 kg)-male
Diet: Meat, such as zebra, antelope, gazelle
Location: Africa, Asia
Lifespan: 15-20 years

The lion is the only big cat that lives in a pack

Male

Lion packs have 2-3 males and 5-10 females and cubs

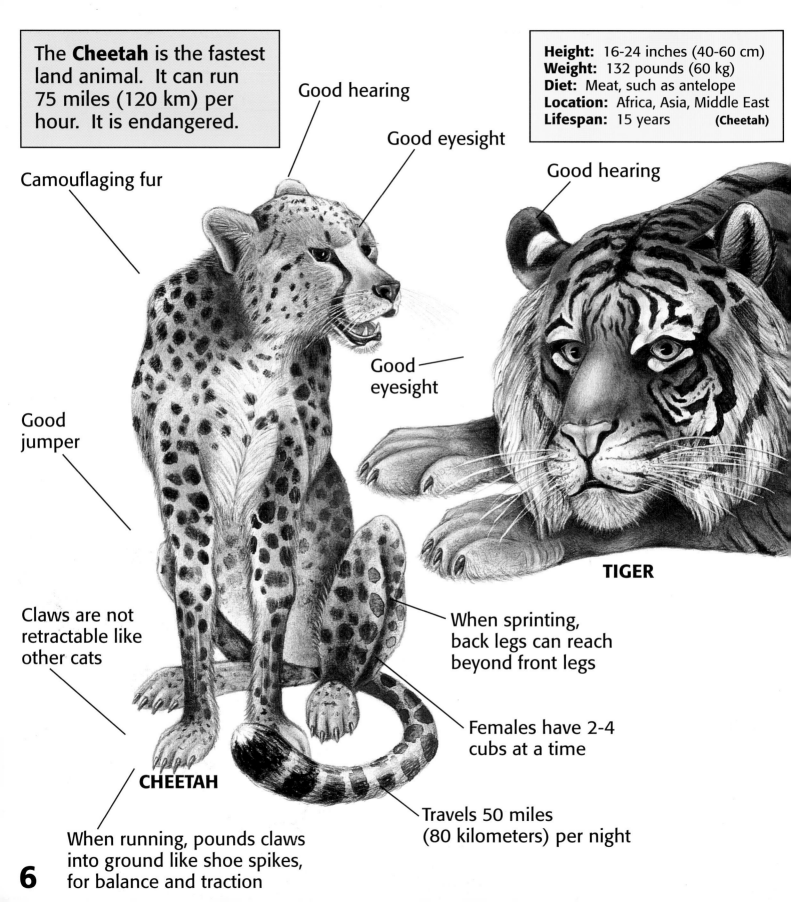

The **Cheetah** is the fastest land animal. It can run 75 miles (120 km) per hour. It is endangered.

Height: 16-24 inches (40-60 cm)
Weight: 132 pounds (60 kg)
Diet: Meat, such as antelope
Location: Africa, Asia, Middle East
Lifespan: 15 years   (Cheetah)

Good hearing

Good eyesight

Good hearing

Camouflaging fur

Good eyesight

Good jumper

TIGER

Claws are not retractable like other cats

When sprinting, back legs can reach beyond front legs

Females have 2-4 cubs at a time

CHEETAH

Travels 50 miles (80 kilometers) per night

6

When running, pounds claws into ground like shoe spikes, for balance and traction

The **Tiger** is the largest and most powerful member of the cat family. It is endangered.

The **Lynx** lives a solitary life in pine forests. It is known for its keen eyesight.

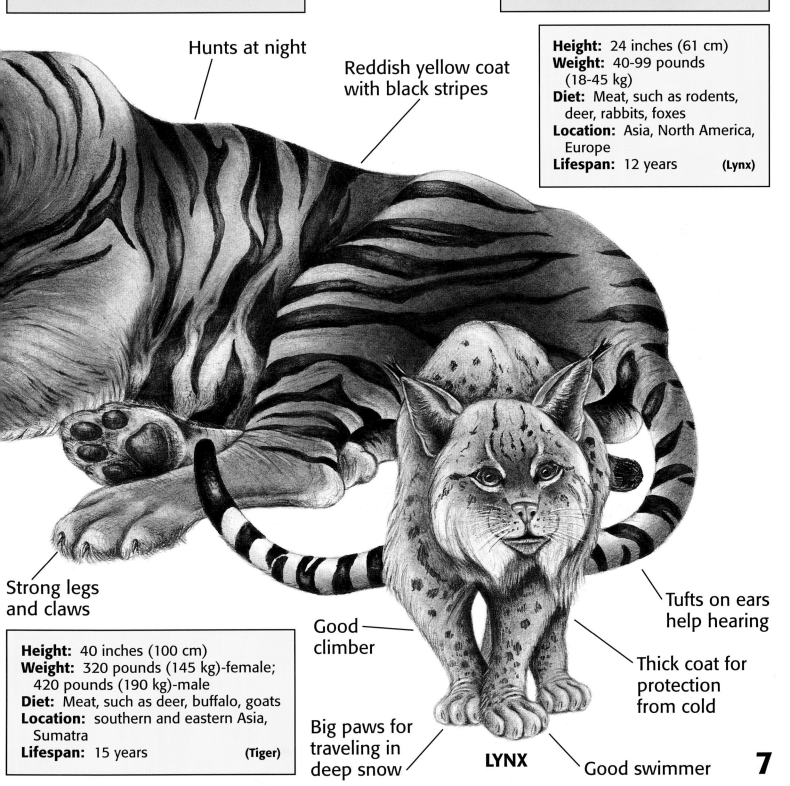

Hunts at night

Reddish yellow coat with black stripes

Height: 24 inches (61 cm)
Weight: 40-99 pounds
  (18-45 kg)
Diet: Meat, such as rodents, deer, rabbits, foxes
Location: Asia, North America, Europe
Lifespan: 12 years   (Lynx)

Strong legs and claws

Height: 40 inches (100 cm)
Weight: 320 pounds (145 kg)-female;
  420 pounds (190 kg)-male
Diet: Meat, such as deer, buffalo, goats
Location: southern and eastern Asia, Sumatra
Lifespan: 15 years   (Tiger)

Good climber

Tufts on ears help hearing

Thick coat for protection from cold

Big paws for traveling in deep snow

LYNX

Good swimmer

7

The **Tanuki**, or **raccoon dog**, lives in family groups in burrows in the ground.

Weight: 11 pounds (5 kg)
Location: eastern Asia, Japan

The **Fox** often plays the part of a clever creature in children's literature.

Height: 15 inches (38 cm)
Weight: 7-31 pounds (3-14 kg)
Diet: Mice, birds, eggs, fruits, rabbits, insects, fish
Location: Throughout world
Lifespan: 8-10 years

Active at night

Likes the cold

Gives birth to 5-8 babies at a time

Good hearing

Good eyesight for hunting

Plays dead when frightened

Mother carries pups in mouth

TANUKI

Sheds year round

Runs at 30 miles (48 km) per hour on short legs

Both parents care for their 4-7 pups

FOX

Height: 38 inches (96.5 cm)
Weight: 45-155 pounds
(20-70 kg)
Diet: Meat, such as deer,
moose, caribou, sheep,
rabbits, ducks, mice, salmon
Location: United States,
Canada, Arctic
Lifespan: 15 years

The **Wolf** was nearly hunted into extinction in the wild.

Strong bite for seizing prey

Good sense of smell

Communicates by howling

Female has 4-7 cubs at a time

Thick coat for warmth

Each pack marks its hunting grounds

Hunts large and small animals, mainly the old, weak, and sick

WOLF

Tail used for steering and keeping warm

Runs long distances at 43 miles (70 km) per hour

9

The **Himalayan black bear** lives alone in hollow trees and in caves. It is endangered.

Active at night

The **Polar bear** lives alone in caves it builds in snowdrifts.

Height: 5.3 feet (1.6 m)
Weight: 650-1,400 pounds (295-635 kg)
Diet: Seal meat, fish
Location: Arctic
Lifespan: 35 years

Growls when afraid

Long hair on shoulders, neck, and throat

Good swimmer

Female has 2 cubs each winter

Good climber

HIMALAYAN BLACK BEAR

Height: 36 inches (90 cm)
Weight: 110-330 pounds (50-150 kg)
Diet: Plants, honey, fruits, plus meat in autumn
Location: southern Asia
Lifespan: 24 years

Webbing between toes helps with swimming

Hair on paws keeps the bear from sliding on ice

POLAR BEAR

Runs short distances at 20 miles (32 km) per hour and swims fast and far

Height: 28-47 inches (70-120 cm)
Weight: 330-715 pounds (150-325 kg)
Diet: Plants, such as berries, roots; and meat, especially salmon, mice
Location: Northern Hemisphere
Lifespan: 15-20 years

Good swimmer

Large head, but small eyes and ears

Waterproof fur to keep skin dry and warm

Teeth designed to eat plants and meat

Runs faster than people; graceful

BROWN BEAR

Female gives birth to 1-3 cubs every 2-4 years

Walks on all fours, but stands to view area

Claws for weapons and climbing, and to dig for mice and roots

Cubs stay with mother 2 years

The **Brown bear** lives in mountains and forests.

11

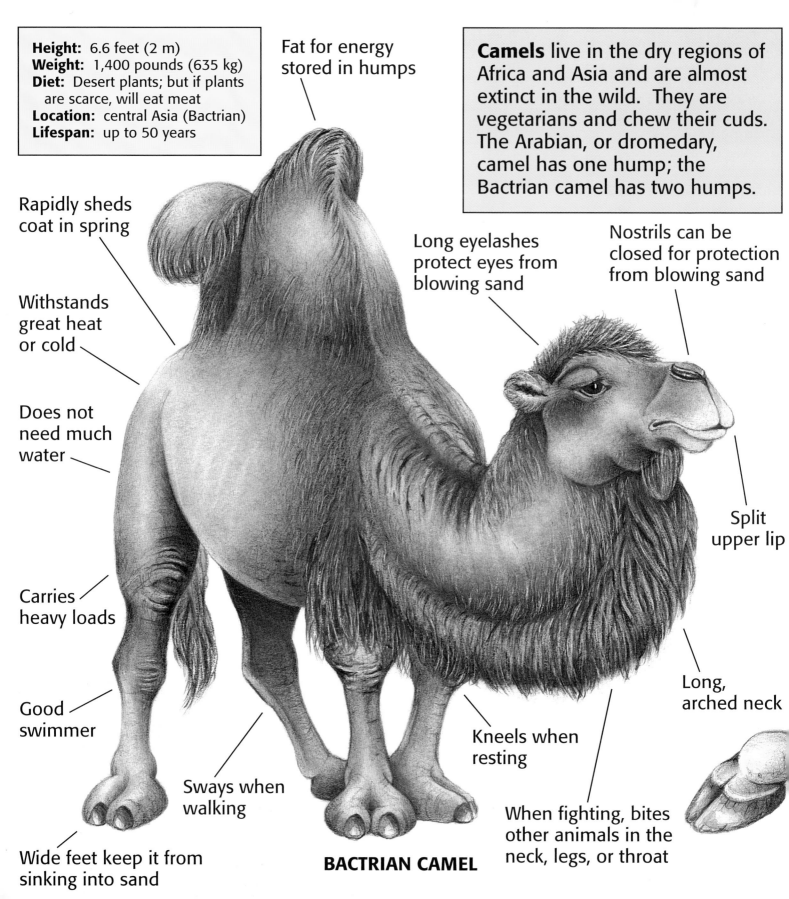

Height: 6.6 feet (2 m)
Weight: 1,400 pounds (635 kg)
Diet: Desert plants; but if plants are scarce, will eat meat
Location: central Asia (Bactrian)
Lifespan: up to 50 years

Fat for energy stored in humps

Camels live in the dry regions of Africa and Asia and are almost extinct in the wild. They are vegetarians and chew their cuds. The Arabian, or dromedary, camel has one hump; the Bactrian camel has two humps.

Rapidly sheds coat in spring

Withstands great heat or cold

Does not need much water

Carries heavy loads

Good swimmer

Sways when walking

Wide feet keep it from sinking into sand

Long eyelashes protect eyes from blowing sand

Nostrils can be closed for protection from blowing sand

Split upper lip

Long, arched neck

Kneels when resting

When fighting, bites other animals in the neck, legs, or throat

BACTRIAN CAMEL

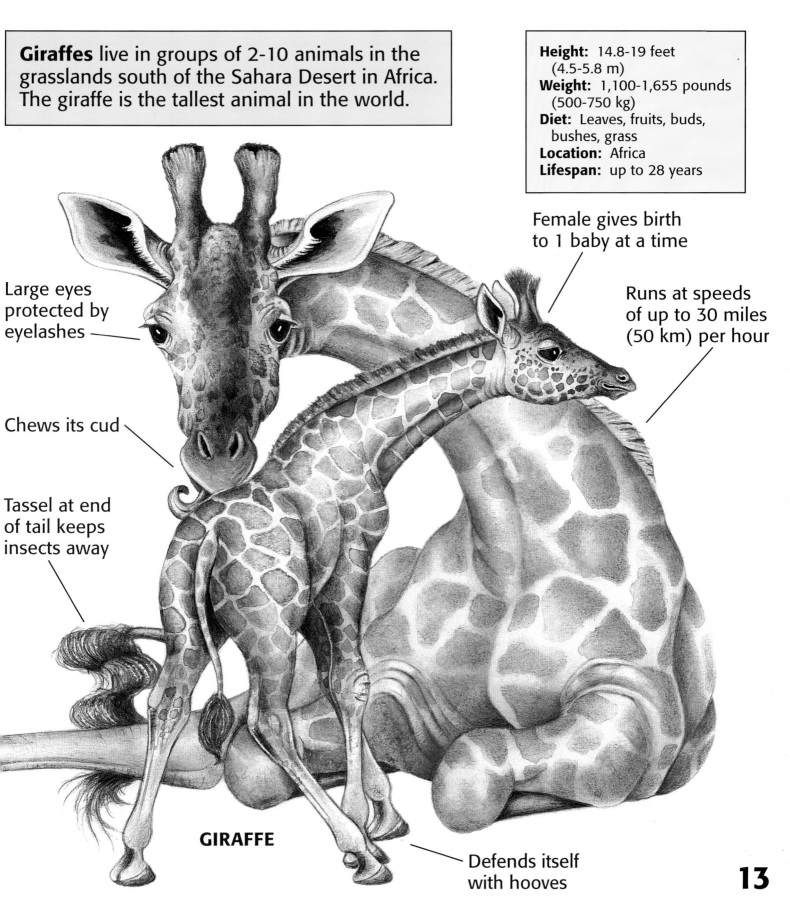

Giraffes live in groups of 2-10 animals in the grasslands south of the Sahara Desert in Africa. The giraffe is the tallest animal in the world.

Height: 14.8-19 feet (4.5-5.8 m)
Weight: 1,100-1,655 pounds (500-750 kg)
Diet: Leaves, fruits, buds, bushes, grass
Location: Africa
Lifespan: up to 28 years

Large eyes protected by eyelashes

Chews its cud

Tassel at end of tail keeps insects away

Female gives birth to 1 baby at a time

Runs at speeds of up to 30 miles (50 km) per hour

Defends itself with hooves

GIRAFFE

13

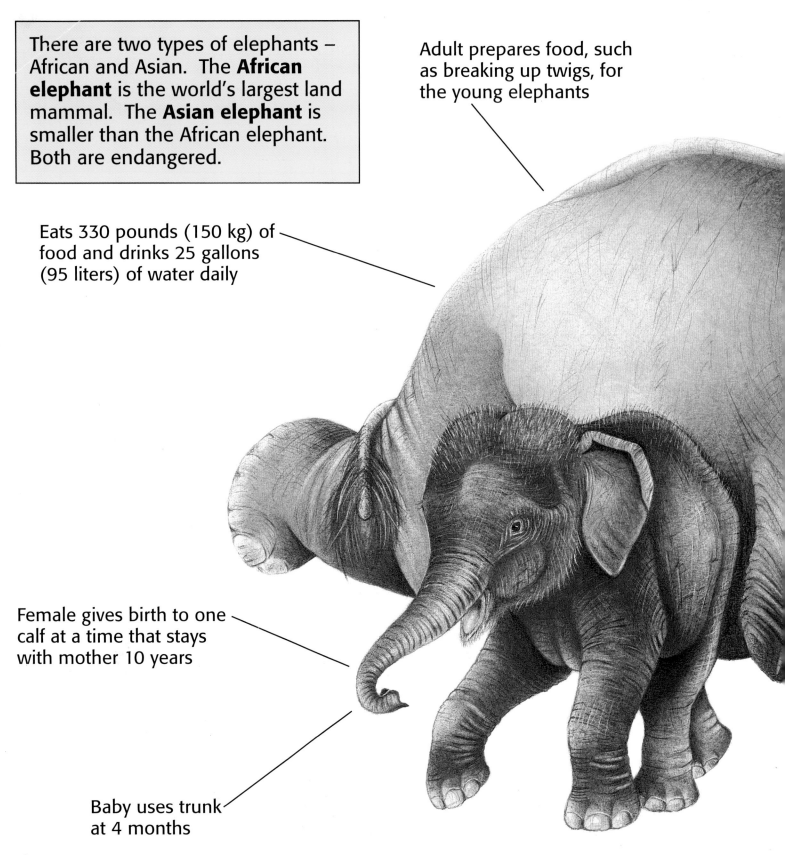

There are two types of elephants – African and Asian. The **African elephant** is the world's largest land mammal. The **Asian elephant** is smaller than the African elephant. Both are endangered.

Adult prepares food, such as breaking up twigs, for the young elephants

Eats 330 pounds (150 kg) of food and drinks 25 gallons (95 liters) of water daily

Female gives birth to one calf at a time that stays with mother 10 years

Baby uses trunk at 4 months

14

ASIAN ELEPHANT

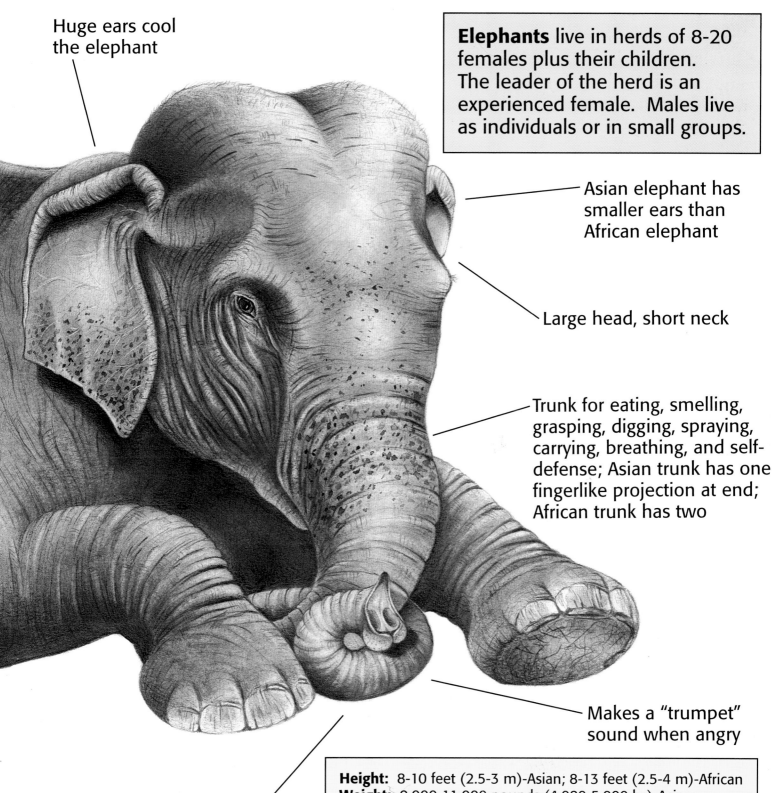

Huge ears cool
the elephant

Elephants live in herds of 8-20
females plus their children.
The leader of the herd is an
experienced female. Males live
as individuals or in small groups.

Asian elephant has
smaller ears than
African elephant

Large head, short neck

Trunk for eating, smelling,
grasping, digging, spraying,
carrying, breathing, and self-
defense; Asian trunk has one
fingerlike projection at end;
African trunk has two

Makes a "trumpet"
sound when angry

Drinks by sucking water
with trunk and then
spraying it into mouth

Height: 8-10 feet (2.5-3 m)-Asian; 8-13 feet (2.5-4 m)-African
Weight: 9,000-11,000 pounds (4,080-5,000 kg)-Asian;
  9,000-16,540 pounds (4,080-7,500 kg)-African
Diet: Plants, such as fruits, tubers, and bark
Lifespan: 30-40 years-Asian; 50-65 years-African

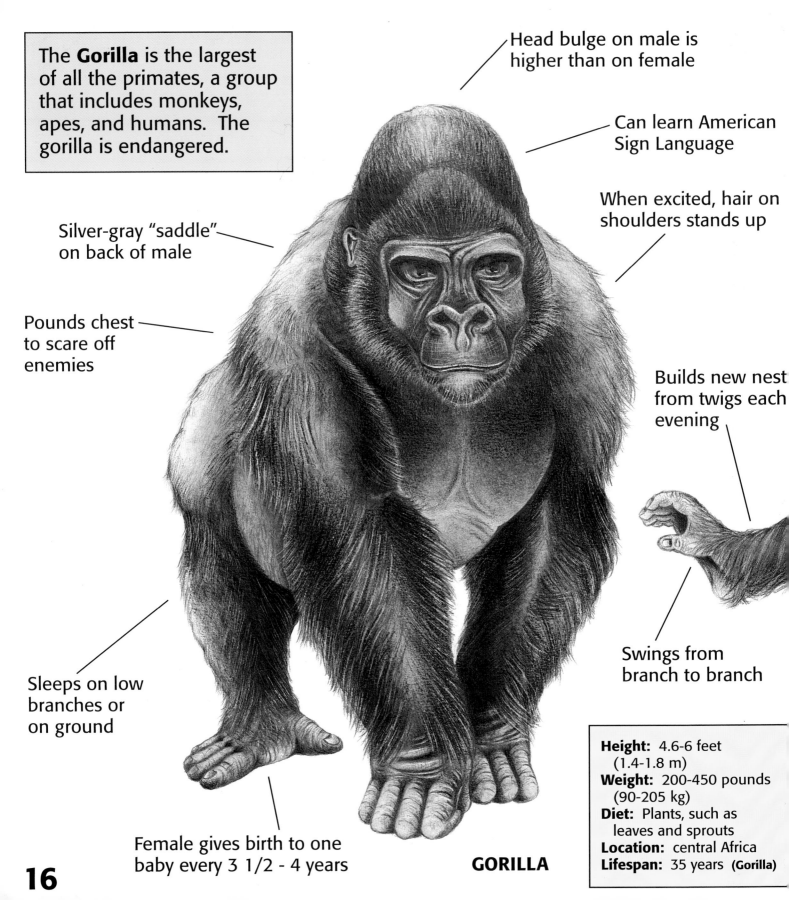

The **Gorilla** is the largest of all the primates, a group that includes monkeys, apes, and humans. The gorilla is endangered.

Head bulge on male is higher than on female

Can learn American Sign Language

When excited, hair on shoulders stands up

Silver-gray "saddle" on back of male

Builds new nest from twigs each evening

Pounds chest to scare off enemies

Swings from branch to branch

Sleeps on low branches or on ground

Height: 4.6-6 feet (1.4-1.8 m)
Weight: 200-450 pounds (90-205 kg)
Diet: Plants, such as leaves and sprouts
Location: central Africa
Lifespan: 35 years **(Gorilla)**

Female gives birth to one baby every 3 1/2 - 4 years

GORILLA

The **Orangutan** is the largest mammal that lives in trees. It is endangered.

The **Chimpanzee** is the most intelligent of all the mammals, second only to humans. It is endangered.

Toes and fingers have nails

Male has beard hair and larger brow and cheeks than female

Height: 4-5.6 feet (1.2-1.7 m)
Weight: 100-150 pounds (45-68 kg)-female; 125-175 pounds (56-80 kg)-male
Diet: Leaves, tree bark, fruits, insects, birds, nuts
Location: Africa
Lifespan: 40-45 years **(Chimpanzee)**

Curious and good natured

Lives with group of 15-120 chimps

Uses tools, such as a stick, to poke into termite nests; licks insects off stick

ORANGUTAN

Female gives birth to one baby every 3-4 years

Feet grasp

Baby stays with mother until 5-7 years old

Height: 54 inches (137 cm)
Weight: 90-110 pounds (40-50 kg)-female; 130-200 pounds (60-90 kg)-male
Diet: Fruits, leaves, flower buds, insects, birds, bird eggs
Location: Borneo, Sumatra
Lifespan: 35 years **(Orangutan)**

CHIMPANZEE

Female gives birth to 1 baby at a time

Runs with finger knuckles on ground

Uses rocks to crack nuts

17

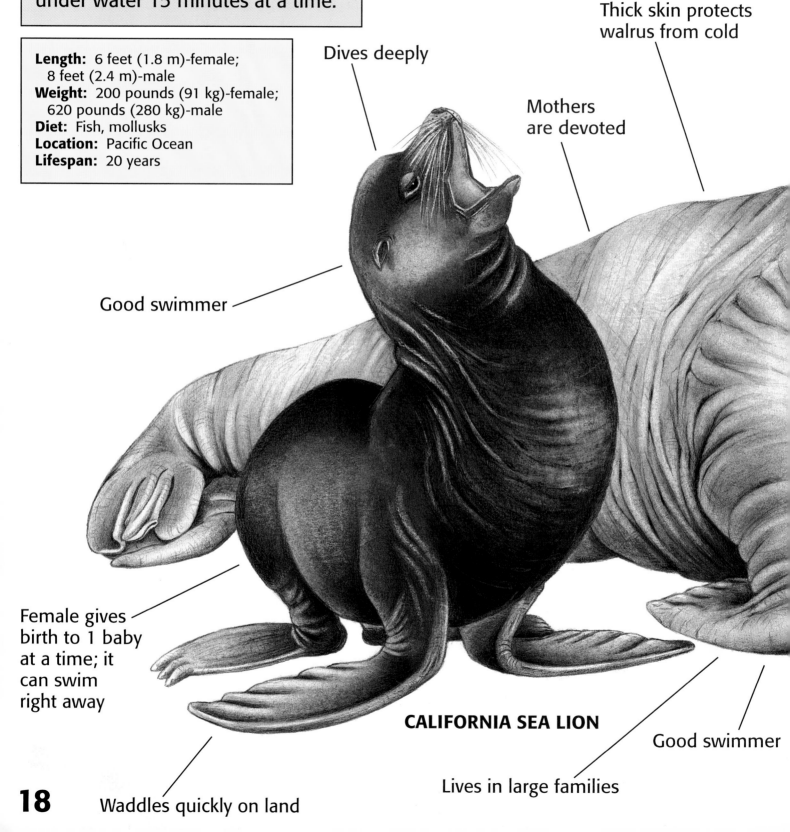

The **California sea lion** can swim under water 15 minutes at a time.

Length: 6 feet (1.8 m)-female;
8 feet (2.4 m)-male
Weight: 200 pounds (91 kg)-female;
620 pounds (280 kg)-male
Diet: Fish, mollusks
Location: Pacific Ocean
Lifespan: 20 years

Dives deeply

Thick skin protects walrus from cold

Mothers are devoted

Good swimmer

Female gives birth to 1 baby at a time; it can swim right away

CALIFORNIA SEA LION

Good swimmer

Lives in large families

18 Waddles quickly on land

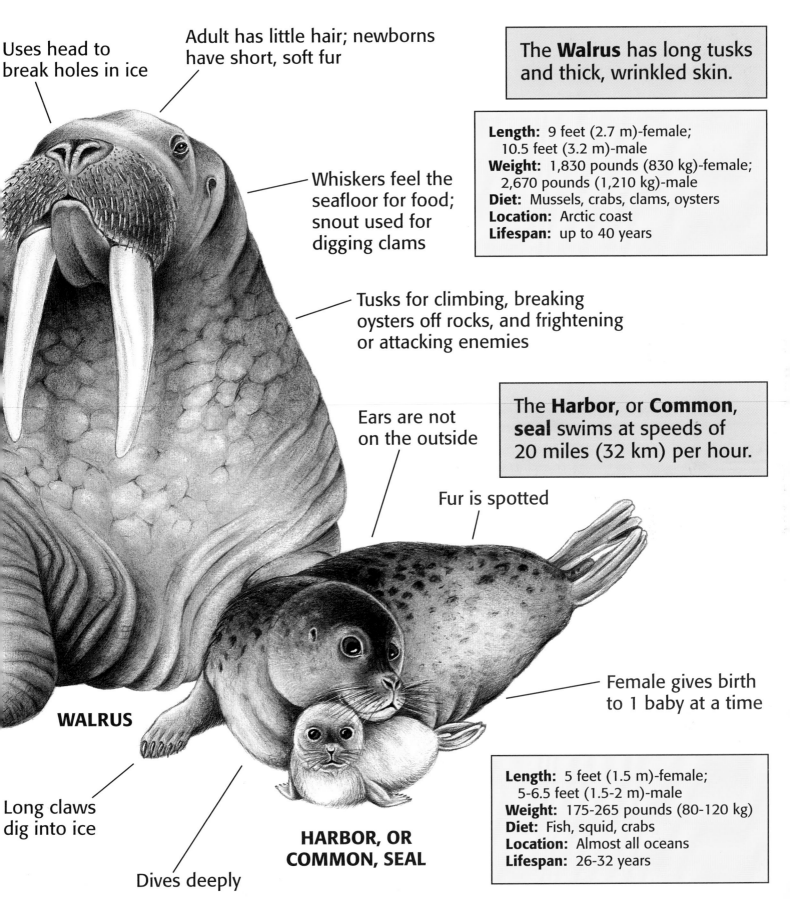

Uses head to break holes in ice

Adult has little hair; newborns have short, soft fur

The **Walrus** has long tusks and thick, wrinkled skin.

Length: 9 feet (2.7 m)-female;
10.5 feet (3.2 m)-male
Weight: 1,830 pounds (830 kg)-female;
2,670 pounds (1,210 kg)-male
Diet: Mussels, crabs, clams, oysters
Location: Arctic coast
Lifespan: up to 40 years

Whiskers feel the seafloor for food; snout used for digging clams

Tusks for climbing, breaking oysters off rocks, and frightening or attacking enemies

Ears are not on the outside

The **Harbor**, or **Common**, **seal** swims at speeds of 20 miles (32 km) per hour.

Fur is spotted

Female gives birth to 1 baby at a time

WALRUS

Long claws dig into ice

HARBOR, OR COMMON, SEAL

Dives deeply

Length: 5 feet (1.5 m)-female;
5-6.5 feet (1.5-2 m)-male
Weight: 175-265 pounds (80-120 kg)
Diet: Fish, squid, crabs
Location: Almost all oceans
Lifespan: 26-32 years

The **Asian rhinoceros** lives alone in grasslands, swamps, and forests. It is endangered.

Thick skin with overlapping folds

Keeps insects, such as flies, away by staying in water

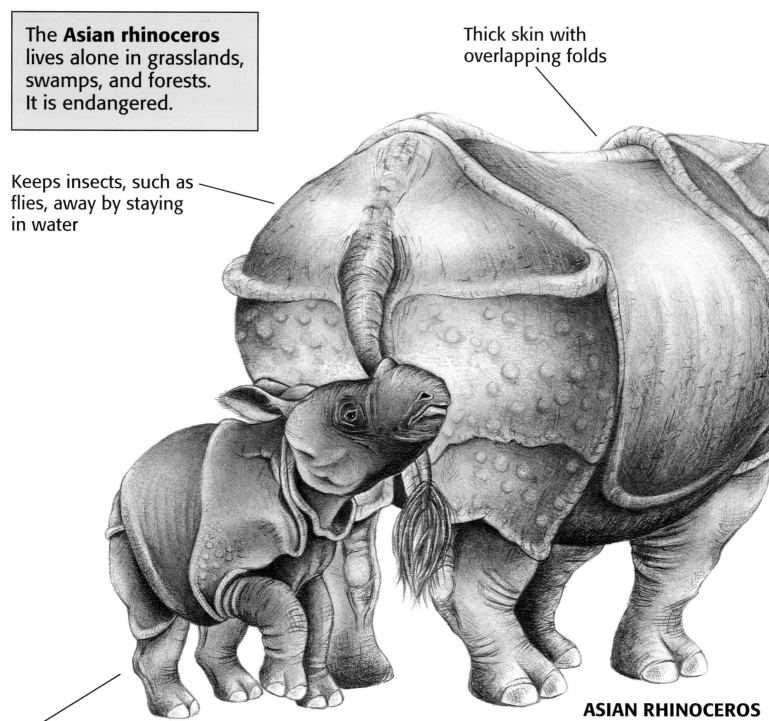

Female gives birth to 1 baby at a time

ASIAN RHINOCEROS

Height: 6 feet (1.8 m)
Weight: 3,530 pounds (1,600 kg)-female;
4,850 pounds (2,200 kg)-male
Diet: Plants
Location: India, Nepal
Lifespan: 45 years

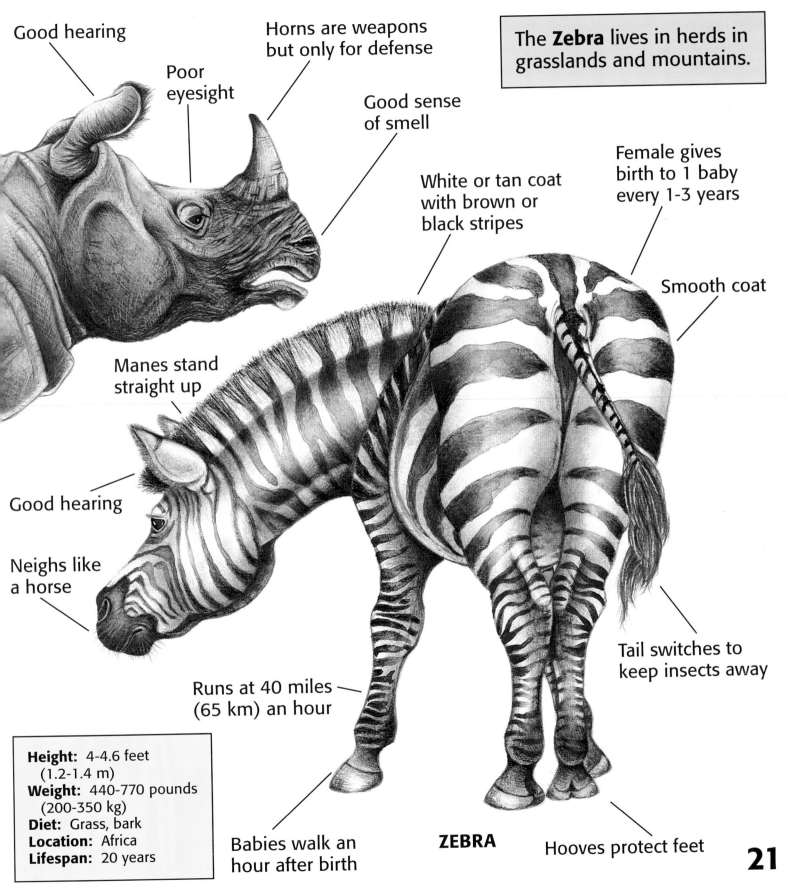

Good hearing

Poor eyesight

Horns are weapons but only for defense

Good sense of smell

White or tan coat with brown or black stripes

Female gives birth to 1 baby every 1-3 years

The **Zebra** lives in herds in grasslands and mountains.

Smooth coat

Manes stand straight up

Good hearing

Neighs like a horse

Tail switches to keep insects away

Runs at 40 miles (65 km) an hour

Height: 4-4.6 feet (1.2-1.4 m)
Weight: 440-770 pounds (200-350 kg)
Diet: Grass, bark
Location: Africa
Lifespan: 20 years

Babies walk an hour after birth

ZEBRA

Hooves protect feet

21

The **Ostrich** is the world's largest bird, but it cannot fly.

Fast runner

Height: 8.2 feet (2.5 m)
Weight: 330 pounds (150 kg)
Diet: Plants, some insects
Location: Africa
Lifespan: 40 years

Wings for steering and stopping when running

Eyes stick out for view of ground

OSTRICH

One ostrich egg weighs the same as 30 chicken eggs

Eggs are laid in hole in sand

Long, powerful legs for kicking attackers

Two toes

Wide toes keep birds from sinking in sand

Parents take turns sitting on eggs

A **Toco toucan** has short wings, and it does not fly well.

Likes taking baths in cold water

Long, light, strong beak

Nests in tree holes

Lives in small flocks in forest

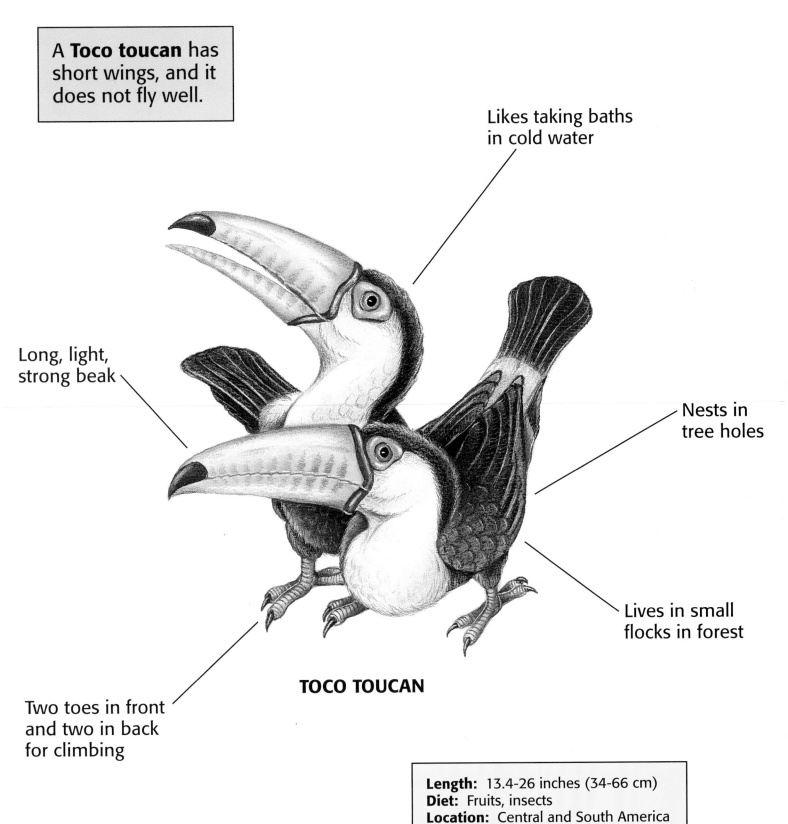

TOCO TOUCAN

Two toes in front and two in back for climbing

Length: 13.4-26 inches (34-66 cm)
Diet: Fruits, insects
Location: Central and South America

The **Red panda** is in the raccoon family. It sleeps during the day in tree branches and hollow logs. It is endangered.

Length: 20-25 inches (51-64 cm)
Weight: 6.6-10 pounds (3-4.5 kg)
Diet: Bamboo shoots, grass, roots, fruits, bird eggs, mice, insects
Location: Himalayas
Lifespan: 13 years

The **Giant panda** is one of the world's most endangered animals. It lives alone on rocky mountain slopes in bamboo forests.

Active at night

Female has 1-4 babies at a time

Lives alone or sometimes in pairs

Two black eyepatches

Sits down flat; tail is cushion

Prefers cold temperatures

Razor-sharp claws for climbing and traveling on ice

Young pandas like to climb

Thick hair on undersides of paws for protection from cold

Holds food with front paws

RED PANDA

Hair on undersides of paws for protection from cold, ice, and snow and to keep from slipping

24

Belongs to the
bear family

Height: 9-12 inches (23-30 cm)
Weight: 11-24 pounds (5-11 kg)
Diet: Insects, worms, crabs, snails,
clams, fish, bird eggs, fruits,
berries, leaves, bark
Location: North, Central, and
South America
Lifespan: 12 years

Female gives birth to
1-7 babies at a time

Active at night

Sleeps during
cold weather

GIANT PANDA

Opposable thumb on front
paws for grasping bamboo

Height: 5 feet (1.5 m)
Weight: 220-330 pounds (100-150 kg)
Diet: Bamboo
Location: China (in mountains near
Tibetan border)
Lifespan: 20-30 years

Skillful paws

RACCOON

Often stands
on hind legs

25

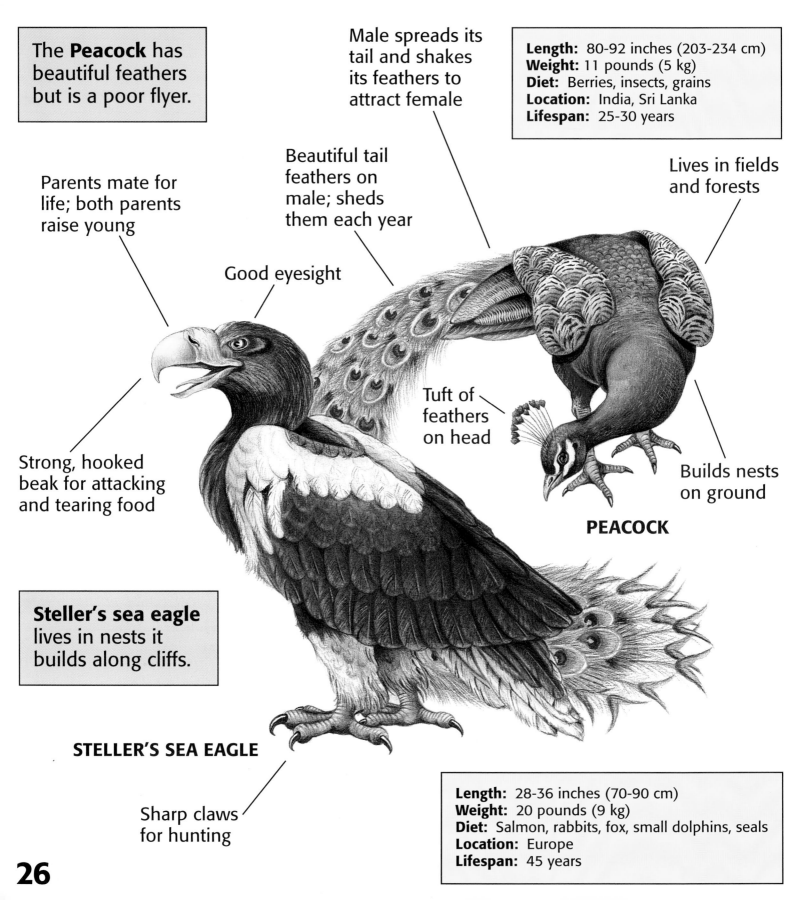

The **Peacock** has beautiful feathers but is a poor flyer.

Male spreads its tail and shakes its feathers to attract female

Length: 80-92 inches (203-234 cm)
Weight: 11 pounds (5 kg)
Diet: Berries, insects, grains
Location: India, Sri Lanka
Lifespan: 25-30 years

Beautiful tail feathers on male; sheds them each year

Lives in fields and forests

Parents mate for life; both parents raise young

Good eyesight

Tuft of feathers on head

Strong, hooked beak for attacking and tearing food

Builds nests on ground

PEACOCK

Steller's sea eagle lives in nests it builds along cliffs.

STELLER'S SEA EAGLE

Sharp claws for hunting

Length: 28-36 inches (70-90 cm)
Weight: 20 pounds (9 kg)
Diet: Salmon, rabbits, fox, small dolphins, seals
Location: Europe
Lifespan: 45 years

ACTIVITIES

1. Make a collage using wildlife pictures you find in magazines.

2. Write to the United States Department of the Interior, Publications Unit, Fish and Wildlife Service, Washington, D.C., 20240, for a list of endangered wildlife. Then write to government officials and express your support of strengthening the Endangered Species Act.

3. Contact a nature organization in your area. Ask how you can become involved in helping to save wildlife.

4. Create a play featuring wildlife puppets with your friends. Decorate a large box with each of the four seasons painted on the four sides. Use the box to present your puppet play to others.

5. Visit the zoo. Make a list of all the animals you see. Which ones are endangered?

6. Visit a national wildlife refuge. Volunteer to help on special projects.

7. Organize a fundraiser at your school or in your neighborhood to raise money to help save endangered animals.

Some organizations working to save wild animals are:

The African Wildlife Foundation
1717 Mars Avenue NW
Washington, D.C. 20036

Jane Goodall Institute for Wildlife Research, Education and Conservation
P.O. Box 26846
Tucson, AZ 85726

World Wildlife Fund
1250 24th Street NW
Washington, D.C. 20037

National Geographic Society
17 and M Streets NW
Washington, D.C. 20036

8. Read books from the library about wildlife. Subscribe to wildlife magazines, such as **Ranger Rick** or **Your Backyard**.

9. Do not buy wild or exotic animals as pets. Also, do not buy fur, bearskin rugs, ivory, or any other products that endanger animals.

10. Educate your friends about respecting wildlife. Ask them not to participate in acts of carelessness or cruelty that could injure an animal.

11. Ask your teacher or librarian about the location of the nearest aquarium, nature/bird sanctuary, and wildlife refuge in your area. Ask the teacher to plan a field trip.

FUN FACTS

1. Elephants actually walk on their toes.

2. Chimpanzees are among the noisiest of the jungle dwellers.

3. The male leader of a group of gorillas is called a "silverback."

4. Rhinoceros horns are made of tightly pressed hairs.

5. Gorillas are peaceful animals.

6. Orangutans are very shy and like to stay in the tops of trees.

7. Adult orangutans live alone.

8. **Orangutan** is the Malay word for "old man of the forest."

9. Lionesses, or female lions, do most of the hunting, but the males eat first.

10. The giraffe has the same number of bones in its neck as other, shorter-necked animals – seven.

GLOSSARY

American Sign Language: a sign language developed for the deaf that features the use of hand signals to communicate.

beak: a bird's hard, pointed mouth.

cud: food that has already been swallowed by an animal, then brought back up into the mouth for chewing.

endangered: in danger of dying out or becoming extinct.

extinct: no longer surviving on Earth.

herd: a group of similar animals that stays together.

hibernate: to rest or sleep for a long period of time, as some animals do in winter.

hollow: empty inside.

hooves: the hard, protective covering of horn on the feet of certain animals, such as horses, zebra, and cattle.

mane: the thick, protective hair on the neck of some animals, such as horses or male lions.

marsupial: an animal that carries its underdeveloped newborn in a pouch outside the mother's body for a time.

pack: a group of similar animals that stays together.

prey: an animal that is eaten by another animal for food.

primates: a group of animals that includes monkeys, apes, and humans.

shed: to lose or drop naturally, such as when an animal loses hair or a tree loses leaves.

tassel: a tuft of hair.

tusk: a long, pointed tooth on the outside of an animal's mouth.

vegetarian: one who eats only plants, fruits, and vegetables.

BOOKS TO READ

Birds. Wings (series). Patricia Lantier-Sampon (Gareth Stevens)
Bison Magic for Kids. Todd Wilkinson (Gareth Stevens)
Camels: Ships of the Desert. John F. Waters (Harper)
Elephants. Animal Families. Barkhausen and Geiser (Gareth Stevens)
A First Look at Owls, Eagles and Other Hunters of the Sky. (Walker)
In Peril. Barbara J. Behm and Jean-Christophe Balouet (Gareth Stevens)
Mountain Gorillas (series). Nichols and Schaller (Gareth Stevens)
Orangutan. Caroline Arnold (Morrow Jr.)
Raccoon Magic for Kids. Jeff Fair (Gareth Stevens)
Walrus: On Location. Kathy Darling (Lathrop, Lee and Shepard)
Where Are My Puffins, Whales and Seals? Ron Hirschi (Bantam Books)
Why Are Animals Endangered? Isaac Asimov (Gareth Stevens)
Why Are Whales Vanishing? Isaac Asimov (Gareth Stevens)
Wolf Magic for Kids. Tom Wolpert (Gareth Stevens)
The Wonder of Black Bears. Beth Karpfinger (Gareth Stevens)
Wonders of Peacocks. Sigmund Lavine (Putnam)
Zebra. Caroline Arnold (Morrow)

VIDEOS

Cougar: King of the Mountain. (Adventure Productions, Inc.)
National Geographic Series: Gorilla; Among the Wild Chimpanzees; Really Wild Animals; Geo Kids.
People of the Forest (The Chimps of Gombe). (Discovery Program)
See How They Grow Series. (Sony)
Sierra Club Series: Orangutan; Tiger, Tiger; We Live With Elephants; Wild Seals.

PLACES TO WRITE

For more information about wild animals, contact the following organizations. Be sure to include a self-addressed, stamped envelope.

Wildlife Conservation International
185th Street & Southern Boulevard
Bronx, NY 10460

National Audubon Society
700 Broadway
New York, NY 10003

**Conservation Commission of
   the Northern Territory**
P.O. Box 496
Palmerston, NT 0831 Australia

Canadian Wildlife Federation
2740 Queensview Drive
Ottawa, Ontario K2B 1A2

INDEX